The World of
Tra

Number Patterns

Andrew Einspruch

Publishing Credits

Editor
Sara Johnson

Editorial Director
Emily R. Smith, M.A.Ed.

Editor-in-Chief
Sharon Coan, M.S.Ed.

Creative Director
Lee Aucoin

Publisher
Rachelle Cracchiolo, M.S.Ed.

Image Credits

The author and publisher would like to gratefully credit or acknowledge the following for permission to reproduce copyright material: Cover Getty Images/Neil Emmerson; p.1 Photodisc; p.4 Photolibrary.com/Alamy/Dave Pattison; p.5 Photolibrary.com/Alamy/Paula Solloway; p.6 iStockphoto; p.7 Photolibrary.com/Alamy; p.8 Picture Media/Eric Pasquier; p.12 (all) Big Stock Photo; p.13 Big Stock Photo; p.15 (both) Big Stock Photo; p.16 iStockphoto; p.17 Big Stock Photo; p.18 Photolibrary.com/Su Keren; p.19 Photodisc; p.20 Photolibrary.com; p.21 Photolibrary.com/Alamy; p. 22 Photolibrary.com/Alamy/Chad Ehlers; p.23 Photolibrary.com/Alamy; p.24 Photolibrary.com/Alamy/Frances Roberts; p.25 123 Royalty Free; p.26 Alamy/Peter Adams; p.27 Photo Edit/David Young-Wolff; p.28 Big Stock Photo; p.29 Shutterstock

Illustrations on pp. 9–11, 14 by Xiangyi Mo.

Teacher Created Materials

5301 Oceanus Drive
Huntington Beach, CA 92649-1030
http://www.tcmpub.com
ISBN 978-0-7439-0879-5
© 2008 Teacher Created Materials, Inc.
Made in China
Nordica.032015.CA21500127

Table of Contents

You Are a Trader   4

Bartering   8

Money   12

Markets   17

The Stock Market   20

Trade Is Everywhere   26

Problem-Solving Activity   28

Glossary   30

Index   31

Answer Key   32

You Are a Trader

Think about the last thing you bought. Maybe it was a toy or some food. Perhaps it was a ticket to a movie.

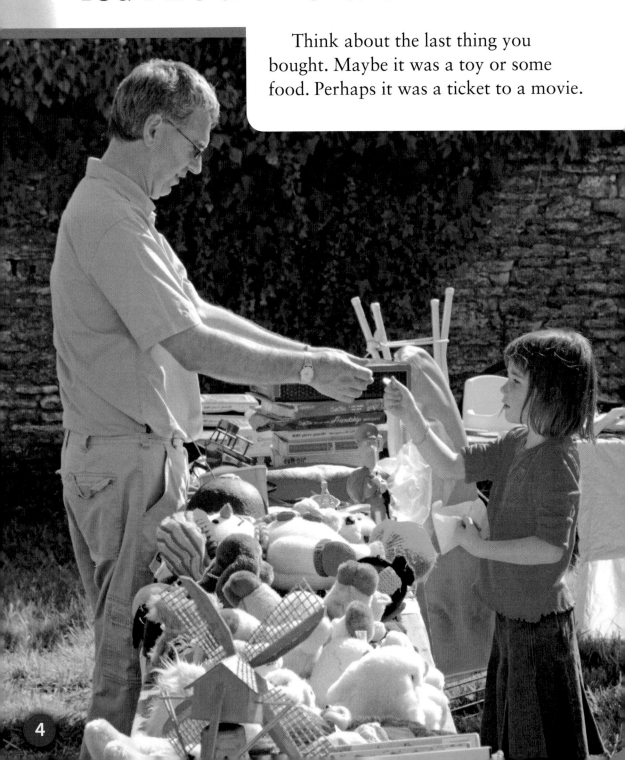

Maybe you swapped something with a friend. Maybe you earned some pocket money. If so, you were involved in trade.

We all buy or sell things. We sometimes swap things. We all take part in the world of trade.

Not Just Swapping!

Think about the types of trading you do with your friends. Maybe you "trade" baseball cards or an apple for your friend's orange. But there is much more to trading than just swapping one thing for another! The word *trade* also covers all kinds of buying and selling.

What Is Trade?

The word *trade* means to buy, sell, or swap **goods** or **services**. Goods are things you can own. Maybe you own a skateboard.

If you bought a skateboard, then you were involved in trade.

LET'S EXPLORE MATH

Skateboards have 4 wheels: 2 at the front and 2 at the back. The table below shows the total number of wheels for different numbers of skateboards. Draw the table below and fill in the blanks.

Number of skateboards	1	2	3	4	5	6	7	8	9	10
Number of wheels	4	8	12	16	20	24				

a. What is the rule for this number pattern?

b. What is the total number of wheels for 6 skateboards?

c. What is the total number of wheels for 10 skateboards?

Services are things people do for you. Some families have newspapers delivered every day. That is a service.

Bartering

People first traded by **bartering**. Bartering is where goods and services are swapped with each other. No money is used in bartering.

These women are bartering salt for corn in Peru.

A Closer Look

I have corn but want beads. You have beads but want corn. We could barter corn for beads. People have bartered for thousands of years. And they still do it today.

LET'S EXPLORE MATH

Julia bartered 3 corncobs for 1 string of beads.

a. Draw the table below and continue the pattern.

Number of strings of beads	1	2	3	4	5	6
Number of corncobs	3	6	9			

b. How many corncobs does Julia need to barter for 6 strings of beads?

Bartering takes a lot of work. First, you have to **bargain**. You have to agree what things are worth. How much corn should I trade for beads?

Second, what if I want your beads but you don't want my corn? We'd have to find someone else who wants corn. She would need to have something that you want—like milk.

Then I could give her my corn. She could give you her milk. You could give me your beads. It's all very tricky!

Money

People had to agree on what things to trade when bartering. They traded things that they all found useful. Many things were used as money.

Long ago, shells, salt, and even pigs were used as money!

Over time, people made **coins** from metals. Metal coins worked well as money. Everyone agreed that metal was worth a lot. Metal coins are easy to carry. They do not wear out or fall apart.

Very early metal coins

LET'S EXPLORE MATH

What belongs on the next 2 lines in this pattern?

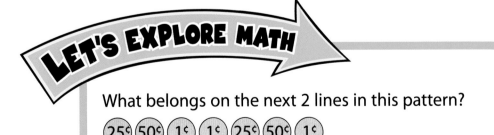

Money Makes It Easy

Money made trading easier. You don't want my corn. So I sell it to someone who does. I take her money for it. Then I give you money for your beads. You can spend that money on something you need.

Bills

Bills make it easy to carry money. A single bill is worth many coins. It would be hard to carry a heavy bag filled with coins all the time!

Coins

Coins let us buy things for less than $1.00. The U.S. dollar is divided into 100 cents. If something costs 25 cents, we can pay with a dollar. We get 75 cents back.

LET'S EXPLORE MATH

This table shows the number of nickels and quarters in 1 dollar.

Number of dollars	1	2	3	4	5	6	7	8	9	10
Number of quarters per dollar	4	8	12							
Number of nickels per dollar	20	40	60							

Draw the table above. Continue the number pattern to find:

a. how many nickels there are in $4.

b. how many quarters there are in $7.

c. how many nickels there are in $10.

Markets

Markets are places where people go to trade. People have been going to markets for thousands of years. The first markets were held outside. The agora was a market in ancient Greece.

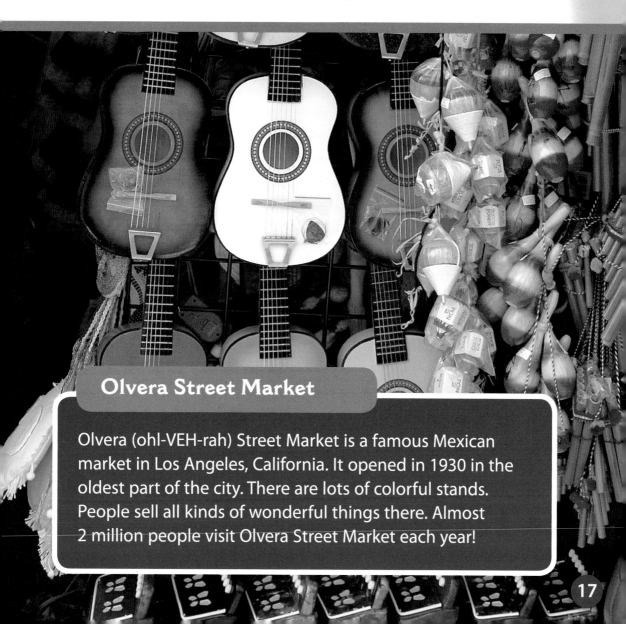

Olvera Street Market

Olvera (ohl-VEH-rah) Street Market is a famous Mexican market in Los Angeles, California. It opened in 1930 in the oldest part of the city. There are lots of colorful stands. People sell all kinds of wonderful things there. Almost 2 million people visit Olvera Street Market each year!

Markets are a good way to trade. People can look around. They can find out what is for sale. Then they can try to get the best deal for what they want.

Floating Markets

In Vietnam, there are "floating markets." The traders sell their goods from boats!

Online Markets

Internet **auction** sites are also markets. You can look at what is for sale. You can still try to get the best deal. But you do not have to walk around. You can do your shopping on a computer.

LET'S EXPLORE MATH

The Online Mall is having a clothing sale. For every $25 you spend, you get $7 off.

Total amount spent	$25	$50	$75	$100	$125	$150	$175	$200
Total amount off	$7	$14						

Draw the table above. Continue the pattern to find:

a. how much money you would get off if you spent $75.

b. how much money you would get off if you spent $125.

c. how much money you would get off if you spent $200.

The
Stock Market

The stock market is a special type of market. It trades shares. Shares are also known as stocks. Shares are small pieces of "ownership" in a company.

You can become one of many owners in a company. You just need to buy shares. The more shares you buy, the more of the company you own!

LET'S EXPLORE MATH

Jada likes to buy shares in the stock market. Each month, Jada buys 50 shares. Write a number pattern to show how many shares she would buy in a year.

Stock Exchanges

There are millions of companies in the world. Some companies are very large. They have many shares. These companies use stock exchanges to buy and sell their shares.

These stockbrokers work at a stock exchange.

Stock exchanges are markets. They bring together people who want to buy and sell company stocks. Stock exchanges trade shares from a list of companies. A company must be on the list to trade its shares there.

This board helps stockbrokers buy and sell stocks.

The NYSE

The New York Stock Exchange (NYSE) is a very famous stock market. It began long ago in 1792.

The highest number of shares exchanged in one day was 3,115,805,723. The lowest number of shares exchanged in one day was 31.

LET'S EXPLORE MATH

A company has a rule that only a certain number of shares can be traded each day. It is a very popular company so it meets the rule every day. Complete the chart below to discover the rule.

Number of days trading	1	2	3	4	5
Shares exchanged	100	150	200		

a. On which day were 150 shares exchanged?

b. How many shares were exchanged on day 5?

c. How many shares would be exchanged on day 8?

Trade Is Everywhere

Trade happens all the time. You can see it everywhere. It is in the lunchroom at school and in the mall. Trade happens at markets and even on the Internet.

Marrakesh market in Morocco

Everyone has something to trade. You might barter with a friend. Every time you buy or sell something, you are playing your part in the world of trade.

LET'S EXPLORE MATH

Gabriel collects trading cards. He wants to buy some new packets of trading cards that will cost him $33.00. He earns $5.50 allowance each week. Draw a table to show how many weeks he would need to save his allowance so he will have enough money to buy the cards.

Cars and Dolls

Dadov toy makers ship their toys around the world. Their most famous toys are trucks and dolls.

The doll makers make 5 dolls in the first hour. As they get better at making dolls, they can make 1 more doll each hour than in the previous hour.

The truck makers make 9 trucks in the first hour. Each hour, they gain 1 more worker. So, they can make 3 more trucks each hour than in the previous hour.

Solve It!

a. How many hours did the doll makers have to work to create 81 dolls?

b. How many hours did the truck makers have to work to create 75 trucks?

c. How many dolls and trucks are made after 10 hours?

Use the steps below to help you solve the problem.

Step 1: Create the chart below. Use a number pattern to work out the number of toys made every hour.

Hour	1	2	3	4	5	6	7	8	9	10
Dolls made	5	6	7							
Trucks made	9	12	15							

Step 2: Create the chart below to work out the total number of toys that the workers have at the end of each hour.

Hour	1	2	3	4	5	6	7	8	9	10
Total dolls made	5	11	18							
Total trucks made	9	21	36							

Glossary

auction—the process of selling something to the person who offers the most goods or money

bargain—the process of getting an item or a price when you are buying or bartering something

bartering—the trading, or swapping, of goods and services without using money

coins—flat pieces of money made out of metal, with different values

goods—things you can buy, barter, or swap

services—works done that help other people

Index

bartering, 8–11, 12, 27

bills, 15

coins, 13, 15, 16

goods, 6, 8

Internet, 19, 26

markets, 17–19, 20, 23

money, 5, 8, 12–16, 27

New York Stock Exchange, 24

number pattern, 6, 9, 13, 16, 19, 21, 25, 27, 29

online markets, 19

services, 6–7, 8

shares, 20–25

stock exchange, 22–25

stock markets, 20–25

trade, 4–7, 8, 10, 12, 14, 18, 20, 23, 25, 26–27

Let's Explore Math

Page 6:

a. Add 4   **b.** 6 skateboards = 24 wheels   **c.** 10 skateboards = 40 wheels

Page 9:

a.

Number of strings of beads	1	2	3	4	5	6
Number of corncobs	3	6	9	12	15	18

b. Julia needs 18 corncobs for 6 strings of beads.

Page 13:

Page 16:

Number of dollars	1	2	3	4	5	6	7	8	9	10
Number of quarters per dollar	4	8	12	16	20	24	28	32	36	40
Number of nickels per dollar	20	40	60	80	100	120	140	160	180	200

a. 80 nickels   **b.** 28 quarters   **c.** 200 nickels

Page 19:

Total amount spent	$25	$50	$75	$100	$125	$150	$175	$200
Total amount off	$7	$14	$21	$28	$35	$42	$49	$56

a. $21   **b.** $35   **c.** $56

Page 21:

50, 100, 150, 200, 250, 300, 350, 400, 450, 500, 550, 600
Jada would buy 600 shares in a year.

Page 25:

Number of days trading	1	2	3	4	5	6	7	8
Shares exchanged	100	150	200	250	300	350	400	450

a. Day 2   **b.** 300   **c.** 450

Page 27:

Number of weeks	1	2	3	4	5	6
Total money saved	$5.50	$11.00	$16.50	$22.00	$27.50	$33.00

It would take Gabriel 6 weeks to save $33.00

Problem-Solving Activity

Hour	1	2	3	4	5	6	7	8	9	10
Dolls made	5	6	7	8	9	10	11	12	13	14
Trucks made	9	12	15	18	21	24	27	30	33	36

Hour	1	2	3	4	5	6	7	8	9	10
Total dolls made	5	11	18	26	35	45	56	68	81	95
Total trucks made	9	21	36	54	75	99	126	156	189	225

a. The doll makers worked 9 hours to make 81 dolls.

b. The truck makers worked 5 hours to make 75 trucks.

c. After 10 hours there were 95 dolls and 225 trucks.